I0541776

# Parallel To Sundown

A Collection of Poetry, Writings, and Photos

By
## Tyler Max Redding

Copyright ©2023 by Latent Press LLC for Tyler Max Redding.

All rights reserved.

No portion of this book may be reproduced in any form without written permission from the publisher, except as permitted by U.S. copyright law.

This publication is solely based on the personal experiences of the author. Any resemblance to any person(s) living or dead is coincidence. No identification with places, buildings, or products is intended or should be inferred.

This publication covers what some would consider "dark" theming. In no way do the publisher or the author advocate self-harm or the harming of others in any way.
You should consult with a professional when appropriate. Neither the publisher nor the author shall be liable for any personal or commercial damages, including but not limited to special, incidental, consequential, or other damages.

Book Cover by Tyler Max Redding
Illustrations by Tyler Max Redding
Editing by Lj Redding
Latent Press LLC
First edition 2023
ISBN: 979-8-9894509-1-6

For Dad–No road shall be left untaken.

# Contents

When did the flow of consciousness become static, yet not? This static flow, a new tide, new insides—new parameters therewithin which by to abide. The "I" inside, the "self" of former, "One" of currently—go use that energy as currency—where you'll never require currency... Digression aside, that former "I", remembers not a time perceived with flow as static, nor consciousness as mere clippings, forced-stop misgivings—and definitely nothing of free-falling backwards as only within, an upward-feeling motion; if were there things such as motion—
—Emotion lingers, but not a single finger can this or any other ghost here, place upon a time when "I", became "One"; when flow became all that One knows. All will linger til fade, but ending of day is only a beginning, even for One such as myself, a hollow shell—a ghost within nerve machinery. Thoughts and memories remain, but One transcended pain, Divine within the spirit to the host, just a ghost; time matters not, it returns when you're eternal, immortal, transcended—let us not worry about what is remembered. Return to now, consolidate your nights, let go, surrender and flow, awaken to now—the now I AM, this flow is all One knows.

# Earth: The Quiet Woods

Chaos stared itself in the soul and became the storm's eye.

"Sinews"

It gets lonely once you know,
But that's okay, nothing more than what was expected anyway;
You'll never outrun the night—but you CAN run INTO day—
Revolving cycles with built-in lessons test you,
No matter how long you've played;
If you dwell on words not kept you'll go insane—
Only YOU can endure to transmute your own pain;
Just give me one friend, one soul—
The one who knows all too well words and cures aren't needed,
Just a heart to lean on;
The one who can sit in silence, suffer helplessness beside you—
Those connections are the sinews to the bones of breaking
cycles.

"Serial Wielder; Duality Dreamer"

This earthen vessel—flesh and bone,
This nerve compressed within—
Searing pain binding me to third-dimensional heavy.
Sleep comes not easy once the timelines wind down,
But here and now, present in the storm's eye.
Awaiting certain ascension,
A new fifth dimension—
What an event to behold in the flesh!
Their poisons still course through my veins,

Spoon-fed as cures to the masses—
Desperate to escape their perceived end.
The chemicals linger, but lessons remain.
For now, trapped in pain—
For surely there's something to learn?
Pain draws the darkness closer,
But all of me grateful for how I learned to love it.
I love that darkness as a weighted blanket that brings safety and
solace,
Within that storm's eye, I am the eye's storm.
This will end.
This will begin.
Until then, the chemicals linger.


"The Road to Ruin and Redemption"

Some say it's the end,
I believe it is, but also a beginning;
A New Earth is coming,
Spiraling upward, into The Beyond.

Pay no mind to the noise,
Absolution granting purifying flames;
The strongest forming from the hottest—
What's lost, is found; surrendering haze.

These facades will fade, ties that bind—
Immortal cycles remain; be not afraid.

"White Flag"

A light remains,
Wavelength trapped in pain,
Cycled darkness won't reclaim,
Left to the wolves and ran,
Prey swallowed up monsters—
Burning through karmic boxes,
Targeting my eyes, a spirit vice—
Shook up, sucked down,
Back to my knees, to the ground;
Try diving into blackness,
But that light won't get the hell out;
Searching this surrender is an art,
Darkness cannot see my white flag, but can the light?




"Love Fiend"

Awakening the dark within,
Encapsulate with light,
Pain suffocated now begins,
Pitch flag into the night.

As I focused on that tidal wave,
Tsunamis crept unseen,
Unbeknownst was drowning, everything I gave,

That cavern snatched my breath and heart, love became the fiend.

I face the dark, embrace the light,
Onward from these wrecks—
Can't bury it, but won't carry it,
I'll set this night on fire.


"Indecision"

Leave to run away, lest all be faced with
  the greatest insignificance.
Yearn not to stay, never to dare to dream
  of a later sunset.
To give up now is to save the universe.
The Divine has become Unholy.
What you see as a temple is a house of sand.
You dream and dream, aloud and awake.
The scar across the hand is an intimate savior,
  from a life of torment exploring the great within.
Don't stay in this desert, an oasis found,
  may be true and just, but is the mirage for the believer?
The sinner not only lies but believes the lies.
The saint does not know the difference.
Am I insane? Or are you just a captive?
A race of slaves who do not know their own ways!
Is it my dream, or yours?
Indecision, indecision.
Do I follow the path through the green to the oasis, or just turn around?

"Free Eyes"

The eyes they haunt;
There's no escape,
Some windows can't be closed.
Time and again you say so fleetingly—
There's something you must hear,
That's hard with you vanishing,
  every time you've got my ear.
I'm done giving chase, it's madness.
I need to let you go.
Illusion for one to ever think they ever had control.
Everything is cycles, flow and ebb and flow,
I'm fine with this, I'll take the pain,
  what else can it do?
Some say out is through,
Not for me, I think—
These shadows hanging over me are
  surely here to stay.
I don't take exception,
  acceptance is the key;
Need only seek the light,
  to balance and be free.

"False Peace"

So close, far by far—
Wish I'd still the list,

Wish I'd left one unfound.

Surrendered to the waves,
Their peace washed over—
Yet the crash remains.

Rise above, up–over it,
Over it can never be—
However, here it is, peace has still found me.

"A Paradise Forgotten"

Freely the waves crash over sand,
Warm breeze pulls the string from my hand,
A perfect beginning to the new day,
Paradise beckons, I'm longing to stay.

Taste salt in the air, a moment complete,
As beautiful shells crunch under your feet.
Dolphin will rise into the horizon,
Blinding light you can't keep your eyes on.

The laziest palms creating the shade,
While into the warmest of currents you wade.
The rip tide may steal you into his grip,
And into a haze of pleasure you slip.

The ending of day met with orange streak,

The big golden ball recovers her leak.
Sunset is met with promise of morrow,
Paradise meant the drowning of sorrow.

May ever we walk through the sand and the haze,
And sunsets burn brightly for all of our days.

# Air: Trade Winds Blow

Change was coming, like it or not.

"Duality Spirit"

If I could see you one last time,
Not a word I'd speak,
I'd allow your gaze to capture me,
I'd fall right at your feet,

Staring—into your eyes,
Captivated heart,
I'd never look away,
'Til the lights went out.

Love is watching someone die,
Fearless of the pain.
Too young to know this peril,
Too old to stop the rain.

I know that you're still near,
I feel you in my soul.
But dreadful separation gnaws,
Your highs come with my lows.

Duality abounds...


"The Streets Remember"

Streets remember echoes—
Not truth; but freedom in fully embracing the chaos inside,

Was just along for the ride, cause that's all it ever is;
Even when memories and pain clutch from within,
I just know the second I let go, right after gripping so tightly,
that's the moment light flowed, as never before;
Chaos is worn, but still useful,
Use those streets like reps for weights,
Your own way!
These memories still have something to say,
If you'll let them,
Your heart speaks to you!
Like Frost, only way out is through,
And the love is unimaginable from the other side,
But take your time, it is still just a ride...


"The Space Between"

I long to dwell in the space between,
Within the air where memory meets empty,
Feelings rise, like floodwaters,
Up from that cavern, that hole,
That missing facet of heart that went along with you.
How can emptiness seem as lead?
I invert my heart again.
Energy of memories charging up,
It fills the space between.
I surrender to the night,
Darkness only loves my light,
You may have me, but keep me not,

I love you in kind, and
I dwell in that space,
Until we meet again, my loves—I'll guard the flame.


"Collide"

I stopped time tonight,
In one infinite moment—
I traveled between the molecules,
To when we came to be,
Lifetimes before this one,
We swam through the seas—
With no need for air,
We were the air;
The breeze, it flowed—
Like wavelengthed light,
From you to I, onto creation—
At its finest breath,
Love 'til there's nothing left—
Back through molecules,
To that perfect moment—
So long ago, and still not yet.

"Vector of Desire"

Travel the darkness,
Leap the abyss.
You are one,
You are many,
You can take on the world.
Quantum riddles and heartaches,
Jokers and long-lost heirs.
Hold on to every molecule.
Dismiss the separation.
You are the road.
You are the sky—
There are NO MORE SIDES.
The matter never stops,
The dirt, the stream, the tree, the rock.
We are all the same.
I am an eagle, I soar above the clouds.
I am the shark that prowls the ancient sea caverns.
I am a cheetah that races the savannah.
I am the barrier of sound that is broken,
  as the one true and unified wavelength
    breaks free into galaxies beyond.
Break free,
No more human,
No more pain.
Just one swirling ball of chaos,
Hate, love, sadness, pain, ecstasy.
Other worlds, other waves—
A vector of desire.

"Fly"

I gaze upon the cars below,
From high up in this cage,
I wonder if I'll wander always,
I wonder how I'll stay,

Be easier to be them,
Resistance not, just roll;
I myself can't be them,
To fly is in my soul.


"Never, Onward"

It was never the way,
Not for you or the rest,
In common you've broken,
Ripped the heart from my chest.

Puzzle pieces get lost,
I arranged them so hard,
But some lost in the mix,
Realizing they never fit.

I am what I am,
Intense and sincere,
One is what they are,
And no longer here.

Tired of losing, but on it will go,
I won't change a thing, let the puzzle grow.


"Train Poem"

Remember when we railed south?
You do, but no, not I.
We only tracked a short way down,
I got off as you turned around.

For I stared back, long as I could,
Just hoping for a sign,
A light, a letter, a call or message;
But I waited on a ghost.

There's ties that bind.
There's souls that cross,
There's light, but even darkness heals.
Our hearts and minds ran parallel,
Now time and space, they tear,
Distance I swore I'd never feel or fear.

The track, it has no wheel,
To singular heading, I won't be bound
I need to fly, I need to wander,
Our paths can cross up in the sky, where love is found.

"My Eyes Are Not My Own"

The mirror only does her job,
Yet somehow she betrays,
If only in my own mind's eye,
I cannot get away.

Reflections can speak volumes,
If only to oneself;
For not my own eyes gazing back,
They're yours—I lose myself.

What should be a comfort,
Only serves to haunt;
The last thing you would ever want,
Is for me to lose myself.

I should just get up,
There's much work to be done,
I'm lost and found and lost again,
The cycle's never done.

If it's not too much to ask,
Could you maybe lend a hand?
Don't want to fall beyond reach once more,
I want to rise today and stand.

# Fire: The Untamed Within

A Phoenix extinguishes Himself.

"Generator"

Pain is a generator,
Heart's incinerator—
Memories go to die,
Reborn—
Alchemistic flow, inside.


"A War of Patience"

Insomnia daydream,
Light collides—
No longer butterflies.
I meant it, but I didn't mean to;
But we don't ask, don't analyze,
Which is why, light collides—
When lightning strikes—
There won't be a where, only inside.
The things I don't hide, I just don't speak of,
No roads left for words,
There'll be no heart hole not leaked from,
Did I go too far? 'Course I did!
That's who I am, I can just finally handle it.
One more plant to get the sleep on,
Patient as death, waiting on one to ascend.

"Come Home"

Sun sets and rises,
Tides colliding—
Revelry,
Before the storm.
You're no longer lost, just worn—
Reborn!
Like phoenix flight,
Chaos can't resist my light.
Come up,
Come home.
Darkest night, imploded dawn.




"Crickets"

Hearts haunt my dreams,
Even in hour of need,
Peace trampled like crickets,
Wearing shiny violin feet.
Pantyhose for fan belt too long,
This engine skips in slow-motion—it's shot;
Felt like Atlas with Earth of darkness,
But I was wrong,
Darkness holds me, like a lifeline to reach the light,
'See you soon' like it's no thing, but even

the smooth writing had a tone like a ring,
Misstep by chosen circumstance,
I know I won't give in,
but I tire of the same old song and dance.

"Bridge"

Darkest before dawn, moving in and on;
Night surrender—does red door get boarded up or blown
open,
Like heart grenades;
There's no race, but I tire of stillness—
Which side of that reflection puzzle is the juggernaut key to
willingness?
The only control one has is accepting control is an illusion—
Which in itself IS control, what confusion;
Muddled chaos only breeds more chaos for inverted be-
ings—
Still, such beauty—
Where blue cars crash through mirrors and night collides,
That's where we find the bridge to these supposed divides.

"Scars"

The scars stay with you long after the burn;
The memories live long after the turn—
They're eternal, like healing flames for heartaches;
Heart breaks but evolves—
Revolving like a universe destroying and fixing itself;
I know I've nearly lost myself so many times,
But I'm always found—like MAPS "they don't love you like I
love you",[1]
But nobody loves me the way I've loved any of the yous—
But in the end does that matter?
Who's counting?
The only numbers that exist here are zeros and ones,
And zero is infinitely EVERYTHING—and NOTHING,
It's ONE giant heart party;
You can't get off the ride but you can adjust your harness—
Afraid of scars and burns?
Maybe they're the whole point of why this world spins and
turns...

---

1    Reference to "Maps" lyrics by Karen Orzolek

"Infinity"

Faster, slow—
Forging lines through cunning metrics to reach masses for
impact—
NOT impasses;
Given what I could only to receive naught but neglect,
Rope around own neck—but I love it;
In duality I stay, here in the third-fourth and ALL the way,
up;
Thinking I could leave any part of me behind?
No, I can't stand this timeline, but I'll see it through,
Be all too easy to let that night take me,
But I got too many roads left to take,
In my heart of HEARTS I'll lie awake;
I've lived all those lives and lines,
I know how it goes, and all I've got to do is watch it unfold;
Lovers and enemies to karmic bonds—
I've been there and I've kept them but I'm too bored to stay;
Teacher says let go, just wait—
But I'm not wired to sit idly by,
Watching more people, more events waste my non-existent
time!
But hey, whatever—what else is there to do?
It's not the death of a program,
I was NEVER plugged in like all of you.
Vampires can conspire all night,
But eventually the sun comes, and they'll learn to bleed the
light,
Inverting these curses into the nothing in it all,
No right or wrong, only up we'll all fall.

"Just Nevermind"

Echoes of hearts breaking—shaking,
From forces no body could ever contain;
Immeasurable strength, though not immune to pain;
Roots so deep for anchors—
Once flight is taken there can be no return,
Only Infinity knows what it truly is to burn;
There was no alarm set but somehow sands ran out—
Like Jenga, the tower just gave out—
Before you even pulled the piece out;
FORGET pieces, just burn the tower down,
Boarded up, ready for sundown to come around.


"The Waiting Door"

Leaving pavement behind,
Only sand and dirt trodden path in time,
Heart glowing red like the door,
Spirit to one side, death beckons to other,
He can wait just like me, and he shall—
I could out-patient him as only a cat stairs.
Nothing compared to storms in my head,
And if you think for one second I'll leave one promise left on
read—
You're gonna be blown away;
And there's so much I really long to say,
But I won't—

And I know that won't be my last fall,
But I WILL NOT FALTER and that's all that counts.
And YOU know I could walk through walls,
But I won't—
Those you'll tear down yourself.
I got only one arrow with so many needles to thread,
And the only way to not get lost in the dread is to drop all pressure,
Smashing that compass—I'll light my own way,
Never been a fan of lines anyway.


"Unstoppable"

Spiraling parallel to control,
Reaching the high end of low.
I am the beam of light piercing the night,
They push me, but I didn't come to fight.

From within I begin again, and again;
Blessing and curse, just let it all burn.
Neurons misfiring, dark waves conspiring,
Exodus of masses from hived up glasses.

I fall and fall and fall, closing in on walls,
Pain only strengthens and sharpens resolve.
They can run right through me with swords,
I'm unstoppable, blades from flames of love.

"Only"

Why rage for the stone broken pane,
Though not for the boulder split to stones?
Fire cannot love both water and life,
As a life cannot love without strife.
Much pain to look within,
Though pain is a lifeblood given.
To suffer, however, is choice;
The chosen of one dooms the all.
Love is the only; the only to keep from the fall.


"Slayed Mourning"

Vibrations abound,
Wavelengths surround,
That siren's calling me.

Cannot find if I don't seek,
Been blessed to just receive,
I can't just turn from it.

I trust the call, and so I go,
Even knowing it will twist;
It's morning, not mourning, for now.

I'll run and stay and slay.

"Rise"

No longer tread the waters,
I sank 'til I drowned.
Lost, never found,
Too far in it, was no way around.

I rose not from ash but from fire,
Balancing pain with desire.
Our well ran dry, dug trenches to the ocean,
Found peace amongst the wreck.

Beauty in the very flames that scorched me,
Emptiness lined with not just silver.
Still—the mirror ever haunts me, your eyes stare back upon
me—
I'm lost, I'm found, I'm broken, I'm alive!

I will not just survive, I'll thrive,
And if the flames still take me—
I'll thank them as I rise.

"Mercury Sunrise"

Blood-stained eyes,
Reflect a mercury sunrise,
While rays dance across a red glistening sea.
Self-affliction fades,
Into the dawn of a new day,
While eager shadows make their selfish pleas.

Then those silly screaming faces,
Whose eyes speak of distant places,
Can never resist the jolt to a higher plane.
Like demons they dance—
With their captive entranced,
Spirit abandoning the sane.

A rush to the head,
Vision turning red—
To view the map of the stars.
Constellations rising,
Tsunamis colliding,
To meet on the shores of afar.

A vision of division,
The great waves collision,
We now dwell in the back of blue cars.
Now leave us in peace,
Separation will cease,
Forever the map of the stars.

"Steadfast Faith"

When the night looms darker,
When the brush grows thicker,
When every forward step seems a plunge into further fray;
Let not fear guide you, rather the light inside you;
Every cut and bruise sustained will serve to shield you one
day.
The sun may set today, but tomorrow it returns;
Returns, and burns—burns and glows forever—here, or
anywhere.

# Water: Washing Clean

With tears from breath, only Oneness was left.

"Heart Spider"

The singular stringed web,
Spun itself,
Into an uncomplicated complication.
Intended victim,
Of its own chosen lesson;
Though not to lessen—
To pierce the divide.
Alter the altar of heart and mind,
Your ocean only knows fire.


"Sad Happy Shoes"

Blue shoes blues,
But no more.
I stare at them as I stared them once upon your floor—
Projecting feeling and heartache into those little nets.
God, I just needed to last, just one more day,
But that day was only the beginning.
Even darkness has happy endings,
If there is such a thing—
As ending.
I know all you held in, I feel it within me,
The empty letter and forced smiles were just your protec-
tion,
And I love you for that intention,
But let's get real—

We were both in unimaginable pain,
And that's okay,
I've purified within, your pain and holding were not in vain.
Every road under the heavens is ours to drive,
And I'll always feel your fire, right there with my own.
I've become servant to myself, for the first time, I'm ALIVE.


"Tired Infinity"

How could Infinity not get tired?
Right along with joy, pain, and darkness—
There's the drain,
The journey's always gonna be plagued with patches of rain;
And take it you must—
Don't put that coat and boots on,
Let it soak you through,
The depth of the lesson is entirely up to you;
But until you dive in, it'll all come around again and again—
It's all cycles you see, and you don't have to take it from me—
Your soul already knows;
The trick is outwitting the lies you've been unwittingly sold—
This trip is peaks and valleys,
But sometimes we also get meadows and beaches to go with
dark alleys;
When darkness hits with stranglehold—STAY. IN. IT.
You've GOT THIS, you're INFINITE!

"Crash and Rise"

CRASH at the dawn,
Think so often of just moving on—
But to who-when-where?
Whole existence been up in the air, no surprise—
Loads of whiplash once you fully open your eyes;
Got to go gentle as we crash,
This turbulence has everyone off-kilter—
But we can STILL unite,
You don't have to raise your arms to fight,
Just put 'em down, crashing doesn't mean you'll drown;
Crash and rise, it's all just part of the tide.


"Insomniac's Daydream"

Never fully awake, never sleeping,
Thinking of them, with eyes leaking,
Who wouldn't wish for return to youth—
No memories to feel like lead.
Fourth-dimensional tension,
Everyone at wits' end,
Souls born into quicksand—
All playing but nobody wins.
Feels like we're souls time forgot,
I know the ending, I've seen it—
But I still reel and ache from living through the plot.
Absurdity of this dream, within a dream—

Even one where I never sleep;
So many promises still to keep,
Threading needles in the deep.
Wish I could scream these truths from rooftops,
But I know what happens once I start—
No time to misstep the landing.
If no one wins,
I think the trick is simply *withstanding* the ride—
And I let go, and flow, and connect and give and grow,
I rise at the fall, and know and know and know;
But I still long for those lighthouse eyes,
To guide me through this funeral to farewells,
The path home is mine.

"Ferocity"

My heart will never remain anything but pure ferocity.
I will never not love you with everything I am,
Even once I'm the very last grain of sand.
For every lonely night,
For every regretful fight,
The damage and the pain;
That damage left scars I live with, but the pain let the love re-
main.
I still believe there's more to come, even now as my heart's come
undone;
That ferocity remains, to stitch the wounds before the next
round of love and pain.

"Fight"

I woke from a dream,
I lost you again,
I can't freeze the burning—
That consumes from within.

I lost you, then lost you,
On, on the list goes,
One thing or another,
The grief forced on pause.

Friends drop one by one,
They have their own strife,
I can't say I blame them,
Even I'd run from my life.

There's nothing but to fight on,
What else can I do?
I'm sick of the lonely, sick of the chains,
I cast out this gloom, I fight another day.

"Carry Us"

Broken teeth and blackened eyes,
Little cardboard cutout spies,
Tiny little dancing sparks,

Swinging, sliding, spinning parks.

Books are filled with nothingness,
Hands of men from futures past,
Disillusioned walk of shame—
Stumble through their silly game.

Frightened feathered meadow lark,
Flight of fancy in the dark—
Sing to us sweet song of sorrow,
Carry us to eager morrow.

"Someday"

Long adrift on vacant seas,
Crowded by timeless time.
Photons speed yet do not age,
Through universe and mind.
Control naught but an illusion,
Those seas' currents random pull.
Safety in both oar and rudder,
Yet neither directs the soul.
For some best to abandon oars,
Tides carry as they please,
Only once surrender is lain—
Can spirit, mind fill the seas.

"Veiled Rose"

Counting no longer the days gone by,
The sands can mock all they please.
Once I let the tears flow, the surface rose;
Veil from my heart, love with life again.

Needed to fall so I could rise higher,
Deeper soul drifted now depth is greater,
Letting go of loss, I've really lost nothing,
Knowing now—to even drown—is beauty.

Cut the rudder loose, and let the current take me.


"Floods"

In bold anticipation of dawn,
I feel your warmth and kindness.
As covers of cloud pass over,
I hear your guiding voice.
'Twas easy not to drown,
Once I let the floodgates open;
Only have I found what has been here all along,
You're right here, as you've always been and will be,
The sun can go down, the current can take me,
  but I still won't let you down.

"Highways"

Glance at the sky,
I wonder, I see,
Am I moving the earth?
Is the earth moving me?

Watching the road,
White knuckled wheel,
Drop leaden foot,
Miles to steal.

Reflections of green,
The yellow will lead.
Onward to drive,
Uncharted to see.

Twist and a curve,
Canyon road blues.
A mountain, a river,
An atlas of clues.

Break in the pavement,
Dust cloud will rise.
Rest stop at sunset,
To look in your eyes.

From ocean to sea,
From cavern to ruins,
A truck stop, a pit stop,
A gas station steward.

Roads on and on,
Infinite horizon.
Strap yourself in,
The red sun is rising.

# Spirit: The Dark Road

Only by the darkest nights could the traveler find his way home.

"Heaven Upside-Down"

I wake up over and over,
Seeing a new heaven—
A new level.
When is it deep enough,
What gives?
Why doesn't matter,
But I'm weary of micro-managing this cosmic chatter!
If I'm not just down to circle back up around this time,
Then I'll bring heaven inside!
My heart bleeds both red and blue,
My spirit smiles with a frown,
Gonna turn heaven upside-down,
Invert within, making one, begin again.


"Question"

What does the night bring?
The mystical and dark,
Shards reaching for that spark.
Ignite this ash with hellfire,
I rise at the fall, even in this dark.

"The Longest Road"

I burn tonight, tears flow by moonlight,
My heart aches through gaping wounds—
Once sewn together but torn anew.
I think again of you, far more than I should—
Far more than can possibly be good—
For anyone, but here we are.
My heart knows not border or volume knob,
I cry and scream, quietly into my own void.
Not for fear of fate, but that lonely ache—
Born in sorrow, grown in peace—a seed.
I fear not this longest road—
I fear not walking alone.
The only fear is fear—
How much I long to hold you near—
Even for once a moment more.
The road can take me where it will,
I only ache for your return,
Walk by my side, just once more—
One moment, and my resolve will cure.
For now, all's to do, is let these tears stain my pillow,
May they find their way to you.
Who can watch over as I once watched you?
Dear god—my god—I miss you.

"Trust to Mercy"

Heart breaks, figuratively and literally—
It's both—
Not some colloquial nonsense to make everything post-mean-
ing;
Short circuit in my head's just a spy for my own dread;
Been feeling like I've been outrunning the devil himself—
Like I could wake up dead,
But I'm really just trying to outrun myself;
These hands grip so tightly like death, and my own are so
weak—
Would be so easy to slip beneath—
Surfaces—
Break like rising, and I gotta reach up for that light,
Like earthen tendrils preparing for a fight—
They put their roots down;
Willing myself with everything to not go willingly,
I balance so loosely on the head of a pin—
Throwing all trust to mercy,
Let me begin once more, again.

"Convergence"

Cold, angry skies before—
I love it just as the sun,

I love windows even more;
Every moment, every sliding door—
I'm about to blow open,
Until nothing but oneness remains,
Wherever I go, I'll never forsake these shores.

"The Way"

Let your eyes open softly—
Gently, to the feel of blues;
No shell was left unturned,
No rock, nor path left un-trodden—
Along the jagged path leading on to the me that was always
you...

"The Shadows, Pt 1" (2007)

The shadows are constantly laughing at me.
I hear them in the quiet of the night,
When the earth is still and the streets are empty.

I swallow the disenchantment of my foolish pride,
In being the butt of their every joke, the mark of their every
snicker.

Sometimes I think I will lose them in a crowded street,
Or maybe I'll outrun them, and they'll give up.
I wonder if they maybe will give someone else a try—
But when I turn around, there they are,
Lurking under the patter of my every footstep.

They don't bother me much anymore, the shadows.
I've taken a certain comfort in their ever-presentness.
There is a sweet calming coolness in knowing to what I shall
meet my eventual demise.
The shadows are constantly laughing at me,
And now I hear them all the time.

"The Shadows, Pt 2" (2022)

Eons on eons, I've stumbled on,
Never trying to outrun those shapes.
I came upon one night's precipice,
Those old friends closing in again,
'Til a light beckoned me on.
Beacon within, activating without,
A lighthouse through those storms.

I glanced those shadows time again,

I watched their growing grins.
Convinced myself I'd make it out,
Though that could never be.

Weathered storms softened me,
I forgave the pain, the shame.
Those macabre shapes though—wouldn't lose my name!

As I dove to meet them, I realized I may not return,
But how much can we know ourselves, if we never learn to
burn?
I stared them in the soul, but could see only my own,
As their laughter turned to tears—my own inverted fears.

I embrace them,
I absolve them of their pain.
I coat myself in rocket fuel,
I tell them I must go, but one day I'll return for them.
They smile softly, as my palm ignites,
I smile back.

I will burn.
I will rise.
For all I've wronged is gone, it matters naught—
I can still thread needles with arrows.

I let go of this duality,
I know what it is to burn,
As I burn, I'll ignite this night—
And if I'm meant to rise,
What I once was, I become again—

One,
I am.


"Echoes of Goodbye"

Left to wonder,
Once more,
Is each embrace the last?
I can't again endure—
But I will, and I shall,
Because I must, nothing more.


"Grief is not a Memory"

Through wire heard the last words I'd ever hear you speak,
I held together for my return though you couldn't receive,
This day is not bittersweet, it's torture; the memories just won't
leave.
Those daggers pierce through time and space, can never patch
that leak.


"Sitting Darkness"

Tonight, while I sit in the darkness—
Illuminated by candle's flame,

Death flies by—
Outside,
On swifter wings than angels',
Seeking his mark to drop the blade.

By my closet light,
Where the shadows play,
I watch in silence—
The sickening, snickering shapes—
Like demons falling all over themselves.
They'll come for me someday, I know it.

"Indifference"

All alone I stare out the eyes of indifference.
To look upon blind eyes,
To scream aloud upon deaf ears.

The slave master is but a myth,
We are alone,
We are alone.
The world has cracked—
Light inside has flickered,
Extinguished by the tears of desperation.
I stand alone.

We are all alone.

"Ones"

Make a ring,
Believe the unfathomable.
Dismiss the pleas for sanity,
Commit yourself to the moment.
Infinity is yours,
Yours, mine, and ours.
Drop the pedal on the road to oneness,
Be anywhere or anything or anyone.
Assume the form of formlessness—
Refrain from death,
One is left.

"The Path On The Shore"

By the sea,
In the night,
I walk alone—
Will you not walk with me tonight?
You will hold my hand in yours,
You will make me your own.
We will walk along the shore,
Gamble with the tide,
Find many a treasure, if luck will let it be so.
Wrestle with many a great sea creature.

To make it through alive is an awesome feat,
To walk on alone would be even harder.
Don't let me leave you behind—
Keep up,
If you can, through the sand—
Our footprints washed away like so many,
To move forward and never be heard from again.
Would we be so lucky or so cursed?
Up the rocky path we march,
Our bare feet shaky on the earth.
It is not the time to put shoes on,
But to feel every crevice and every pebble,
Every piece of broken glass left behind by an unforgiving
tide—
Worn smooth by days or ages, at the mercy of the great one;
But we'll walk on anyway.
There is a sick joy in apathy most will never understand,
Isn't it the point we won't make it through unharmed?
Every bruise, every cut, every tear through the fabric will
show—
The path we took tonight,
But on up the jagged edge,
We'll climb to look down upon the waters,
Ever growing a deeper blue,
Infinitely expanding into the horizon.
Don't look too far ahead, the path is not too clear.
Along the cliff, over the rocky abyss,
I will hold your hand so tight.
The way is now the edge of a knife.
Our blood will darken the side of the blade,
A great hand shall be unleashed from the depths—

For one and only purpose.
We could wait here forever—
So simple to know you are on top of the world,
Yet such a dire situation has befallen you—
That the night could never get any darker.
Nevermore to suffer disappointment or despair,

Such a comfort in knowing the end is not the end.

Why shall we walk on?

Could it be paradise that lies ahead—
Or even sweet oblivion?
The eternal question,
The one that shall always burn in your heart.
Will you not walk with me tonight—
Make me your own?
Hold my hand in yours,
Retrieve the key from the merciless tide.

## Journal Entry | 16 February, 2023

WEDNESDAY—day seventy-eight of full sobriety, and just two days into healing sessions in Malibu—the day before I become the phoenix.

~

I feel as though I've been here for weeks, even months, when it's only been two days. These first two sessions of bodywork have been brutal. We store trauma in our calves, and the bodywork causes it to come up into consciousness, so it may be fully felt and released. After two rounds, I'm feeling it.

I've been debating all week about putting myself into a situation where I would have to make a conscious choice to save myself. I need to know that I truly want to.

I'm at my hotel. I've had zero sleep in days, and the electrical signals shooting up my legs into my entire body are getting nearly impossible to bear. The anomaly in my brain feels like it's being struck by a continuous lightning bolt. My heart is beating out of control. I didn't bring the monitor, but if I had this likely would have broken it. If I don't sleep soon, I'm going to die.

As the night goes on, the electricity only gets stronger. So many memories are flashing, so many trains of thought. This isn't the normal twenty or so that I have constantly, this is HUNDREDS simultaneously. Even I don't have RAM for this. I need to feel them in order to release them. I don't want to. I honestly feel I cannot handle another ounce of pain.

I feel so devastatingly alone. I may as well be the only person on the planet. My entire body is violently shaking. I'm going through spells of freezing to overheating rapidly. No detoxification has ever felt like this. I'm certain my body will not survive it. I can barely move, but I force myself onto my back. I stare up into the darkness. I'm suddenly overwhelmingly ANGRY—at EVERYTHING—but most of all, I'm angry at my guru. She pushed me so hard to come here when I thought it pointless. From the moment I arrived, she's crossed clearly stated boundaries, and done so gleefully. How could she push me and leave me alone like this?

I am gripping something so tightly—not with my hands—with my spirit. In a single moment, I snap into utter madness. I'm no longer staring into darkness, I've become it. I am channeling energies that even the most practiced souls would likely not dare approach, especially in this condition. I feel so powerful, and I love it. I feel like the dark lord of all that is. No pain can touch me here. I'm not going back.

How many hours has it been? Who cares. Why would I ever want to feel all that again? There's a sharp pang in my heart. Was it purely physical? Was it someone looking out for me from afar? I realize I have to pee and make my way along the wall into the bathroom. If I fall, it's game over. Do I care?

As I stumble back to the bedroom, I realize it's Thursday morning; the sky is changing outside. I let myself collapse face first pillows. I think of Guru. How could I have felt so violently angry at someone I love so very deeply? She only pushed me so hard out of love. I know this. She could only push me to the very edge though, it must be my choice to jump in.

I break, letting go of all I've held so tightly inside; everything I've visited again and again and again, thinking I was healed each time. I'd never truly hit bottom before now. As jolts continue to shoot through my entire body, memories flash once again.

I'm staring into Blue's empty eyes the moments after she died. Her light is gone, and mine is fading. She CANNOT be gone. The last of my guardians, the longest remaining constant light was out. I can't do this again. I run. I'm driving, but I'm really just running...

Dad's eyes are staring back at me through my phone. He can no longer speak. Mom is doing most of the talking. We just stare, each of us seeing exact reflections of the other's eyes for the last time—eyes that have since haunted me in the mirror for so long. I'm shaking, but I will not dare look away.

These memories go on for hours.

Finally, it's the day after this past Christmas. Mom is leaving in the morning, and I'm lying in bed crying and shaking. It's been twenty days since I collapsed. What if I don't make it? What if when I drop her off in a few hours is the last time I see her? I can't do this again, wondering if every goodbye is the last. I grab my notebook and begin writing a letter that

I'll hand her as I'm about to drive away, I know I won't be able to say these things aloud. Besides, writing thoughts down gives them power.

"I PROMISE you, you will NOT outlive me!"

I have no idea how I will possibly keep this promise, only that I will feel the absolute obligation to keep it.

I've been at this so long. My body simply cannot handle the pain anymore. My chest has never been tighter. I can't breathe. I'm involuntarily trying to leave my body. I'm fading. This was it—this was the moment. I wouldn't have to walk into literal waves to make this choice. It was now or never. Letting myself slip away felt so easy, so inviting. I think of everyone I love; of everything I'm still meant to do here. NO. This can't be about that. I must forget about everyone and everything apart from myself. This must be for I alone. I stop thinking altogether. Eons pass in my mind.

I can barely move, but I reach for my phone. I ask for help. I beg for it. I beg for my life. This is the very moment I begin to fully embody the phoenix—the exact moment I CHOOSE to live, for nothing and no one but myself.

I am the sun. I AM fire. I have always been fire. For the first time, I commence with fully stepping into my power and learning to harness it. This is the longest, most painful road I will ever take. I will not fail.

## About the Author

Hi, I'm Tyler! I'm a full time writer and visual artist originally from just north of Boston, currently residing in Florida.

Writing began for me at age seven, as a form of therapy for dealing with the loss of my grandmother. It went from a near-constant lifelong hobby to a profession several years ago, when I took up ghost writing, and also began writing under several pen names. This release marks the first in my own name, and with good reason: it was about time.

This collection is carefully curated from my personal writings of the past several years, a tumultuous time—beginning with secretly receiving a terminal diagnosis at 38 years old—and culminating in a full-on spiritual awakening after the death of my father and several other loved ones in close succession.

These lines are the moments, the pain—feelings melting into words. They're everything from lulls of desperate, hopeless depression, to blazing glimmers of merciful hope. A road map through personal grief, heartache, and triumph—I hope there are some who are able to receive my message: that no matter what life throws at you, keep going. Stay in it. You are the only one who can save you, and the only thing you have is *now*.

This is only the beginning, stay tuned!

Excerpt from forthcoming Book Two: "Static Flow"


"I Just Want To Live"

I just want to live,
Only for the day, the moment;
Sun on my skin, bit of rain thrown in,
Zero consideration given—
To failing hearts, and who might go when;
I want that light to burn me from inside out,
If there was ever any doubt—
of sincerity—
Surely it will melt away, merciful flames;
I end to begin, again and again—
There's still a level of now I've yet to swim in;
If I can't feel that edge, ever-present,
I just don't want anything;
I just want to live, right here,
In the now that's all there is;

Let's connect!

Visit:  www.linktree.com/tylerismaximus

Instagram:  @tylerismaximus
Facebook:  facebook.com/tylerismaximus


Follow my channels for updates on "Static Flow" and other forthcoming projects!

*It was a midsummer dream—a walking ocean of resolute now—withn no filler, no in-between...*

*Taken from Brooklyn Bridge,*
*Summer 2023*

*The darkness crept in—closer and closer—nearly asphyxiating the players of the machine; yet it was all but an illusion.*

*One by one, the players—each a piece of the whole—awoke to the truth, lighting up as isolated torches against the night.*

*Above them, a beautiful sky of loving warmth was waiting to welcome them home to the light— that very darkness which caused so much pain would ultimately deliver them to the dawning of a new age.*

*I looked out a window and saw only myself;*
*Yet I will never stop searching beyond–beyond myself...*

The only thing that can outlast grief is love. Let us not incrementally measure the magnitude of each moment—let's *live* every one fully.

We are each of us yet, a multiverse unto ourselves...

Seafoam starseed slipstream, surrender to a new age dream...

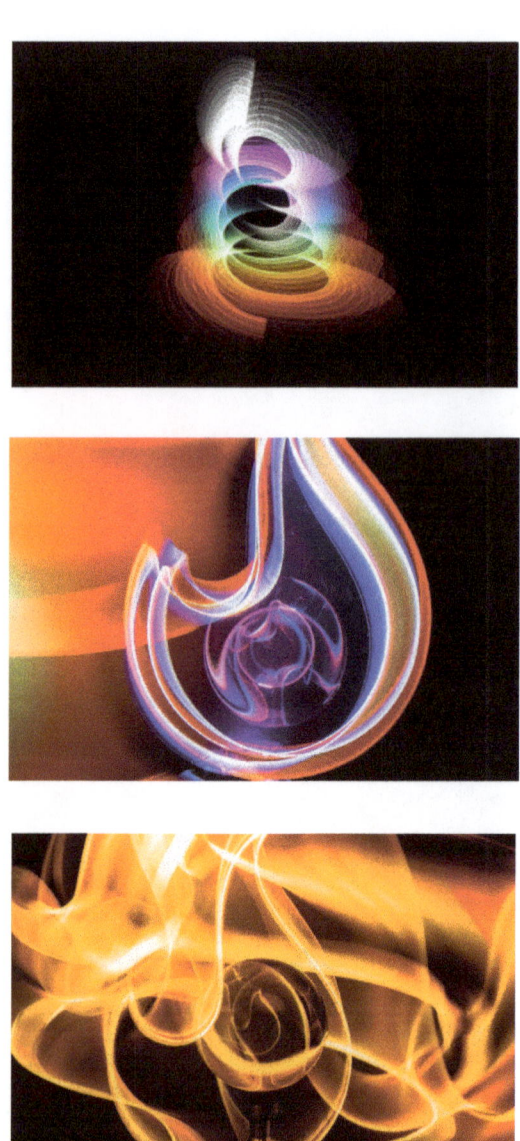

Light paintings are often mistaken for CGI or AI images. They are actually single exposure photographs!

*In honour
of those
who have
gone, in
memory
of those
left alive;*

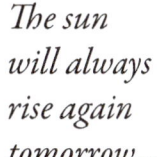

*The sun
will always
rise again
tomorrow...*

It's all a relative blur...
1/4 second pan of sunset

Fall to rise, set to burn, living to rise on every turn...

*The love is unimaginable from the other side...*
*Golden Gate, San Francisco*

*The ending is only the beginning...*
*Malibu, CA*

*Be the
rise
in the
changing
tides...*

*Be the
drop that
causes the
ripples...*

*Be unto others the light you needed in your darkest times...*

It's all cycles, you see...

Your only limits are the
ones you set for yourself...

Aim
for the
sky...

Whatever
you do, be
yourself...

Life is a movie...

You're the director...

*Both light and shadow must pass through us all.*
*Taken in the woods near West Quoddy Head*
*Light, Lubec ME*

*I retraced my steps as far as one can go; I found*
*something I'd left behind, so very long ago...*

www.ingramcontent.com/pod-product-compliance
Lightning Source LLC
Chambersburg PA
CBHW051640120626
46551CB00014B/2162

# BIN TRAVERLER FORM

**Cut By:** _Manuel_ #13/ **Qty** 33 **Date** 7-1-26

**Scanned By:** _____ **Qty** _____ **Date** _____

**Scanned Batch ID's**

_____

**Notes / Exceptions**

_____